GUITAR NOTEBOOK

The Smart Practice
Journal for Guitar

This book is dedicated to all our students and readers—local and abroad. May we continue to teach and inspire one another.

Published by **GuitarIQ.com**

Copyedited by Allister Thompson

Proofread by Dan Foster

Illustrated by Jasmin Zecchin

Contents

Get Your Free Online Bonus Now!

This book comes complete with free online bonus material. We've compiled a companion website to enhance your reading experience. Extras include audio examples, backing tracks, bonus downloads, and more!

Get your free bonus content at: **www.guitariq.com/gn-bonus**

Introduction

The *secret* to becoming a better guitar player isn't really a secret. The truth is so simple, it's easy to miss out on its full impact. Improvement is just the process of working on things you can't do until they're no longer an obstacle. Focus on what you want to achieve, work out what's getting in the way, and begin clearing a path. It's as uncomplicated as that!

Sounds good in theory, right? So why do we often hit plateaus in our guitar playing? For most of us, the problem isn't a lack of resources or enthusiasm–it's a lack of direction. Think about it: How do you get from A to B without knowing where B is? Some of the biggest hurdles in effective practice are simply the result of poor planning. If you have no idea what to practice, when to practice, and how long to practice, is it any wonder that practice feels unproductive?

Today, learning tools are more advanced than they've ever been; we live in the age of apps, podcasts, ebooks, and online courses. Just because learning is more accessible, however, doesn't mean it's easier. With all the information you'll ever need at your fingertips, organizing your time and focusing on what's important has never been more valuable! Despite the constant threat of information overload, the key to getting better remains refreshingly simple: Write it down. Work on it. Get results.

This practice journal is born from years of playing experience coupled with key insights from experts in the field of learning and skill development. Not only will this planner help you avoid common roadblocks, but it will also introduce a proven framework for accelerated improvement. The system outlined in this guide will help you practice smarter, develop your skills better, and achieve your playing goals faster. If you want to make your practice count, this little notebook may be the most valuable (and possibly least expensive) guitar accessory you'll ever own!

Things You Should Know

I know...you're probably not in the habit of reading instructions. We've all done it! That said, it's worth making an exception here. To get the most out of this notebook, you need to understand the basic framework we'll be using. Let's start by introducing the "S" word. You guessed it: *structure*. As musicians, it's easy to react negatively to the idea of structured practice. After all, we're the masters of improvisation; making things up spontaneously is what we do! If you want the quickest route to playing success, however, having a clear system for getting there is key.

Exercise, Learn & Create

This entire handbook is structured around three main concepts: Exercise, Learn, and Create. Anything you practice will fit into one of these three categories. The important thing isn't what each category is *called* but what each category represents. Here's an overview of how these concepts apply to your weekly practice schedule:

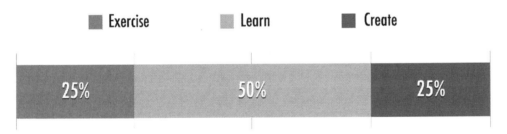

- **Exercise:** This first portion of your practice (roughly 25%) involves things like drills, warm-ups, and workouts. It focuses on the content you already know. The purpose is to hone and consolidate the skills you've already learned.

- **Learn:** This middle portion of your practice (roughly 50%) involves things like skill development, refining your repertoire, and working on new material. It focuses on the content you're currently working on. The purpose is to continue expanding the edges of your playing ability.

- **Create:** This final portion of your practice (roughly 25%) involves things like improvising, writing, and exploring new ideas. It focuses on the content you'll discover. The purpose is to apply and experiment with the things you've been working on.

Obviously, these are general guidelines. You'll quickly realize that one category will inevitably cross over into another. This is a good thing! What you discover will fuel the things you're working on; the things you're working on will develop into what you know—it's all part of the natural learning cycle. The point isn't to enforce strict boundaries but to introduce a simple and effective framework for structuring your time.

Tasks & Goals

Within the Exercise, Learn, and Create framework, things are divided into two basic objectives: *tasks* and *goals*. Tasks outline the action you want to take; goals specify the outcome you want to achieve. The benefit of this is twofold; it tells us what to focus on and lets us track how we're progressing. For the best results, we need to be as specific as possible with our objectives. For example, while resolving to "learn that new song" is helpful, it's not very informative. Instead, look at the song, break it down, find your weak spots, and outline the parts needing the most attention.

Once you've chosen a task, it's extremely beneficial to establish goals that represent a small challenge—something just beyond your current reach. Use your goals to highlight any potential problem areas and give yourself something to work toward. For example, rather than planning to loop an exercise for 3 minutes, try adding an element of risk. See if you can loop the exercise 10 times without making a mistake; each mistake means having to start again! Ultimately, the more intentional you can be with your tasks and goals, the more helpful you'll find them.

How It Works

This handbook is divided into four sections comprising 13 weeks each. You can use these sections alongside a school or college calendar or simply align them with months/seasons of the year (whatever makes most sense to you). The important thing is this structure breaks down the year into smaller sections. This provides regular intervals to reflect on how you're progressing, reassess where you're headed, and establish new short-term goals over the next quarter.

Each week lets you map out your practice game plan. As discussed, this includes outlining the tasks you want to work on and what you're hoping to achieve. You can also track your time spent and make note of any problem areas you encounter. Under each of the Exercise, Learn, and Create categories, you're limited to planning just three tasks for the week. Simplifying your objectives in this way helps clarify what's important and avoids information overload.

Note: Although it's best to fill in all three tasks for each section, this doesn't mean each task must be practiced every day. It's an outline of what you'd like to focus on over the week.

As a suggestion, take 5-10 minutes each weekend to plan your practice for the week. (If you find this difficult at first, just fill in any blank spaces during the week as you go.) This framework allows you to vary your daily practice based on what feels most appropriate. You want to have enough flexibility that your practice doesn't become stale but enough structure that you stay on course. Remember, be as specific with your tasks and goals as possible. The clearer your idea of what you want to improve, the more effective your practice time will be.

Finally, at the back of this notebook you'll find sections labeled "Recommended Reading," "Recommended Listening," and "Recommended Viewing." You can use these pages to compile an inventory of helpful resources that you come across throughout the year. This list might include things like books, magazines, blogs, websites, tutorials, courses, songs, albums, movies, apps, and podcasts. Even if these don't directly relate to your immediate practice goals, don't underestimate the importance of things that inspire and excite you.

Using This Handbook

Now that we've outlined how to use this practice journal, let's take a more detailed look at each section of your weekly planner.

Exercise: Drills, Warm-Ups & Workouts

The *Exercise* portion of your practice represents roughly the first 25% of your time. It's a chance to get your head (and fingers) in the game. Depending on your skill level, this section could comprise a wide range of tasks, from basic finger drills and picking exercises to advanced scale workouts. The purpose is to continue building familiarity, strength, and dexterity with material you already know.

Warming up, however, doesn't mean *mindlessly* playing through familiar shapes and patterns. It involves both your head and your hands. As with all practice tasks, the best warm-ups have an element of challenge—something to work toward. Even with familiar material, being mindful of your weaknesses and having clear practice goals is essential. Below are a few examples.

Beginner Example

Tasks	Goals
1) Warm up with basic finger exercises (Book 1, page 4)	– Practice slowly and play notes cleanly – Aim for 5 repetitions without a mistake
2) Warm up with basic picking exercises (Book 1, page 8)	– Focus on picking accuracy – Aim for 5 repetitions without a mistake

Intermediate Example

Tasks	Goals
1) Warm up with pentatonic exercises (Book 2, page 20)	– Loop through all 5 positions in sequence – Practice horizontally across top 3 strings
2) Warm up with arpeggio exercises (Book 2, page 35)	– Keep each note consistent in volume – Aim to progress 10BPM by end of week

Learn: Songs, Theory & Technique

The *Learn* portion of your practice represents roughly the middle 50% of your time. As such, it forms the core focus of your practice session. (That's why it's important to spend the most time on it!) This section could include numerous tasks like learning songs and licks, developing new techniques, building your chord and scale vocabulary, working on theory and ear training, or refining your repertoire. The purpose is to keep pushing the limits of your ability and understanding.

The things you work on here should align with your overall playing goals. This part of your practice is where you continue shifting the goal posts forward (one note at a time!). Remember to avoid vague or ambiguous directions; it's crucial to think about the specifics you need to work on. Below are some examples.

Beginner Example

Tasks	Goals
1) Work on major scale position 1 (Book 1, page 15)	– Memorize this pattern by end of week – Practice this scale in all 12 keys
2) Work on verse and chorus of Song 5 (Book 1, page 23)	– Focus on timing when changing chords – Keep to the strumming patterns outlined

Intermediate Example

Tasks	Goals
1) Work on solo section of Song 2 (Book 2, page 30)	– Concentrate on pitch when bending strings – Practice speed-picking lick at 1/2 speed
2) Work on ear training (Disk 2)	– Focus on recognising intervals and triads – Aim for 80% accuracy by end of week

Create: Improvise, Write & Experiment

The *Create* portion of your practice represents roughly the final 25% of your time. Here the focus is on discovery. Anything goes in this section, so get creative! Some suggestions might be jamming over backing tracks, experimenting with new concepts, reworking old ideas, or creating your own compositions. The purpose is to apply the things you've been working on in a creative context.

Learning new material can be mentally and physically draining. (It's not always fun working on things you can't do yet!) This last part of your practice is a great way to reward yourself and ensure that you finish on a positive note. As with the other two categories, outlining clear objectives is essential for getting the most from your time. Below are a few examples.

Beginner Example

Tasks	Goals
1) Improvise over major jam tracks (Disk 1)	– Create a melody using the major scale – Contrast the sound of different notes
2) Write short progression based on Song 5 (Book 1, page 23)	– Reorder chords to make new song idea – Try out different strumming patterns

Intermediate Example

Tasks	Goals
1) Experiment with licks from Song 2 (Disk 2)	– Write 3 riffs based on ideas from solo – Explore speed lick using different scales
2) Improvise over Dorian jam tracks (Disk 3)	– Practice navigating all 7 scale positions – Focus on melody, space, and phrasing

Track Your Progress

In addition to the main sections of your practice schedule, each week you're also able to track your progress. This includes recording your daily practice time and making note of specific issues you come across during the week.

The chart below lets you record the minutes spent practicing each day. It allows you to track your consistency over the life of your practice journal. Simply cross out each day you practice and total the minutes spent (not including breaks). Obviously, the time you spend is up to you. As a general guide, however, a good starting point would be 30-40 minutes per day for beginners and 60-90 minutes per day for intermediate players. Below is what a normal week might look like.

Example

Day	S	M	T	W	T	F	S
Time	45	25	30	30	30	—	40

Note: The stopwatch symbols provided ( ) indicate when to shift focus within the Exercise, Learn, and Create framework. While these depict a 60-minute cycle, remember that they represent the percentage of time allotted to each section, not the amount of time you should spend.

Finally, the section "Focus Points" can be used to list any problem areas you (or your guitar teacher) notice while practicing. This could include things like issues with technique, bad playing habits, things you keep forgetting to do, and other general reminders. Below are some examples of observations you might jot down when practicing.

Example

- Focus on the beat and be conscious of not rushing

- Remember, accuracy is more important than speed

- Concentrate on not pressing so hard on the strings

- Try to keep your fingers in closer to the fretboard

- Stop tensing up and remember to breathe normally

Reflect & Plan

Before you get started, take a moment to assess where you're at, where you're headed, and what's getting in the way.

Where are you at?

Based on the last 3 months...

What are the main things I've been working on?

_____

_____

_____

_____

_____

_____

What can I do now that I couldn't do before?

_____

_____

_____

_____

_____

_____

What are the key things I still need to work on?

_____

_____

_____

_____

_____

Where do you want to go?

Looking forward...

Where do I want my playing ability to be in 5 years?

_____

_____

_____

_____

_____

_____

What would I like to be able to do in 12 months time?

_____

_____

_____

_____

_____

Which achievements are most important in the next 3 months?

_____

_____

_____

_____

_____

_____

What's holding you back?

If I'm honest...

What are the key issues stopping me from getting better?

\
\
\
\
\

What are the main excuses I use for not taking action?

\
\
\
\
\

What will I regret most if I never reach my long-term goals?

\
\
\
\
\

How will you move forward?

In the next 3 months...

What key changes do I need to make?

_____

_____

_____

_____

_____

_____

Which central tasks do I need to focus on?

_____

_____

_____

_____

_____

_____

What tools and resources do I need to help me?

_____

_____

_____

_____

_____

_____

The 1st Quarter

Welcome to the first phase of your practice domination. If you've read the instructions closely, it's time to get started!

Week 1

Exercise

Tasks	Goals
1)	
2)	
3)	

Learn

Tasks	Goals
1)	
2)	
3)	

⏱ Create

Tasks	Goals
1)	
2)	
3)	

Day	S	M	T	W	T	F	S
Time							

Focus Points:

_____

_____

_____

_____

_____

_____

_____

_____

Week 2

☼ Exercise

Tasks	Goals
1)	
2)	
3)	

☼ Learn

Tasks	Goals
1)	
2)	
3)	

⏱ Create

Tasks	Goals
1)	
2)	
3)	

Day	S	M	T	W	T	F	S
Time							

Focus Points:

Week 3

⏰ Exercise

Tasks	Goals
1)	
2)	
3)	

⏱ Learn

Tasks	Goals
1)	
2)	
3)	

⏱ Create

Tasks	Goals
1)	
2)	
3)	

Day	S	M	T	W	T	F	S
Time							

Focus Points:

Week 4

Date: _____ / _____ / _____

Exercise

Tasks	Goals
1)	
2)	
3)	

Learn

Tasks	Goals
1)	
2)	
3)	

⏱ Create

Tasks	Goals
1)	
2)	
3)	

Day	S	M	T	W	T	F	S
Time							

Focus Points:

Week 5

Date: _____ / _____ / _____

Exercise

Tasks	Goals
1)	
2)	
3)	

Learn

Tasks	Goals
1)	
2)	
3)	

⏱ Create

Tasks	Goals
1)	
2)	
3)	

Day	S	M	T	W	T	F	S
Time							

Focus Points:

Week 6

☼ Exercise

Tasks	Goals
1)	
2)	
3)	

◖ Learn

Tasks	Goals
1)	
2)	
3)	

⏰ Create

	Tasks	Goals
1)		
2)		
3)		

Day	S	M	T	W	T	F	S
Time							

Focus Points:

Week 7

Date: _____ / _____ / _____

☼ Exercise

Tasks	Goals
1)	
2)	
3)	

☀ Learn

Tasks	Goals
1)	
2)	
3)	

⏱ Create

Tasks	Goals
1)	
2)	
3)	

Day	S	M	T	W	T	F	S
Time							

Focus Points:

_____

_____

_____

_____

_____

_____

_____

_____

_____

Week 8

⏲ Exercise

Tasks	Goals
1)	
2)	
3)	

⏲ Learn

Tasks	Goals
1)	
2)	
3)	

⏱ Create

Tasks	Goals
1)	
2)	
3)	

Day	S	M	T	W	T	F	S
Time							

Focus Points:

Week 9

Exercise

Tasks	Goals
1)	
2)	
3)	

Learn

Tasks	Goals
1)	
2)	
3)	

☼ Create

Tasks	Goals
1)	
2)	
3)	

Day	S	M	T	W	T	F	S
Time							

Focus Points:

Week 10

☼ Exercise

Tasks	Goals
1)	
2)	
3)	

☼ Learn

Tasks	Goals
1)	
2)	
3)	

⊙ Create

Tasks	Goals
1)	
2)	
3)	

Day	S	M	T	W	T	F	S
Time							

Focus Points:

Week 11

Exercise

Tasks	Goals
1)	
2)	
3)	

Learn

Tasks	Goals
1)	
2)	
3)	

⏲ Create

Tasks	Goals
1)	
2)	
3)	

Day	S	M	T	W	T	F	S
Time							

Focus Points:

Week 12

Exercise

Tasks	Goals
1)	
2)	
3)	

Learn

Tasks	Goals
1)	
2)	
3)	

⏱ Create

Tasks	Goals
1)	
2)	
3)	

Day	S	M	T	W	T	F	S
Time							

Focus Points:

Week 13

Exercise

Tasks	Goals
1)	
2)	
3)	

Learn

Tasks	Goals
1)	
2)	
3)	

⏱ Create

Tasks	Goals
1)	
2)	
3)	

Day	S	M	T	W	T	F	S
Time							

Focus Points:

Reflect & Plan

Well done—you've earned a break! Let's revisit the key questions for staying focused in your practice time moving forward.

Where are you at?

Based on the last 3 months...

What are the main things I've been working on?

_____

_____

_____

_____

_____

What can I do now that I couldn't do before?

_____

_____

_____

_____

What are the key things I still need to work on?

_____

_____

_____

_____

Where do you want to go?

Looking forward...

Where do I want my playing ability to be in 5 years?

What would I like to be able to do in 12 months time?

Which achievements are most important in the next 3 months?

What's holding you back?

If I'm honest...

What are the key issues stopping me from getting better?

_____

_____

_____

_____

_____

What are the main excuses I use for not taking action?

_____

_____

_____

_____

_____

What will I regret most if I never reach my long-term goals?

_____

_____

_____

_____

_____

How will you move forward?

In the next 3 months...

What key changes do I need to make?

_____

_____

_____

_____

_____

_____

Which central tasks do I need to focus on?

_____

_____

_____

_____

_____

_____

What tools and resources do I need to help me?

_____

_____

_____

_____

_____

_____

The 2nd Quarter

Welcome to the second phase of your practice domination. Well, what are you waiting for? Let's get started!

Week 1

Exercise

Tasks	Goals
1)	
2)	
3)	

Learn

Tasks	Goals
1)	
2)	
3)	

⏱ Create

Tasks	Goals
1)	
2)	
3)	

Day	S	M	T	W	T	F	S
Time							

Focus Points:

Week 2

Exercise

Tasks	Goals
1)	
2)	
3)	

Learn

Tasks	Goals
1)	
2)	
3)	

☺ Create

Tasks	Goals
1)	
2)	
3)	

Day	S	M	T	W	T	F	S
Time							

Focus Points:

Week 3

⌛ Exercise

Tasks	Goals
1)	
2)	
3)	

⌛ Learn

Tasks	Goals
1)	
2)	
3)	

⏱ Create

Tasks	Goals
1)	
2)	
3)	

Day	S	M	T	W	T	F	S
Time							

Focus Points:

Week 4

Exercise

Tasks	Goals
1)	
2)	
3)	

Learn

Tasks	Goals
1)	
2)	
3)	

⏱ Create

Tasks	Goals
1)	
2)	
3)	

Day	S	M	T	W	T	F	S
Time							

Focus Points:

Week 5

⏱ Exercise

Tasks	Goals
1)	
2)	
3)	

⏱ Learn

Tasks	Goals
1)	
2)	
3)	

⏱ Create

Tasks	Goals
1)	
2)	
3)	

Day	S	M	T	W	T	F	S
Time							

Focus Points:

Week 6

Exercise

Tasks	Goals
1)	
2)	
3)	

Learn

Tasks	Goals
1)	
2)	
3)	

⏲ Create

Tasks	Goals
1)	
2)	
3)	

Day	S	M	T	W	T	F	S
Time							

Focus Points:

Week 7

Exercise

Tasks	Goals
1)	
2)	
3)	

Learn

Tasks	Goals
1)	
2)	
3)	

⏱ Create

Tasks	Goals
1)	
2)	
3)	

Day	S	M	T	W	T	F	S
Time							

Focus Points:

_____

_____

_____

_____

_____

_____

_____

_____

_____

Week 8

☼ Exercise

Tasks	Goals
1)	
2)	
3)	

☐ Learn

Tasks	Goals
1)	
2)	
3)	

⏲ Create

Tasks	Goals
1)	
2)	
3)	

Day	S	M	T	W	T	F	S
Time							

Focus Points:

Week 9

Date: _____ / _____ / _____

☼ Exercise

Tasks	Goals
1)	
2)	
3)	

☾ Learn

Tasks	Goals
1)	
2)	
3)	

⏱ Create

Tasks	Goals
1)	
2)	
3)	

Day	S	M	T	W	T	F	S
Time							

Focus Points:

Week 10

☼ Exercise

Tasks	Goals
1)	
2)	
3)	

☼ Learn

Tasks	Goals
1)	
2)	
3)	

⏱ Create

Tasks	Goals
1)	
2)	
3)	

Day	S	M	T	W	T	F	S
Time							

Focus Points:

Week 11

Exercise

Tasks	Goals
1)	
2)	
3)	

Learn

Tasks	Goals
1)	
2)	
3)	

⏱ Create

Tasks	Goals
1)	
2)	
3)	

Day	S	M	T	W	T	F	S
Time							

Focus Points:

Week 12

Exercise

Tasks	Goals
1)	
2)	
3)	

Learn

Tasks	Goals
1)	
2)	
3)	

⏱ Create

Tasks	Goals
1)	
2)	
3)	

Day	S	M	T	W	T	F	S
Time							

Focus Points:

_____

_____

_____

_____

_____

_____

_____

_____

_____

Week 13

Exercise

Tasks	Goals
1)	
2)	
3)	

Learn

Tasks	Goals
1)	
2)	
3)	

⏲ Create

Tasks	Goals
1)	
2)	
3)	

Day	S	M	T	W	T	F	S
Time							

Focus Points:

Reflect & Plan

Congratulations, you've made it halfway! Let's take another break to reassess how things are going and how you can keep improving.

Where are you at?

Based on the last 3 months...

What are the main things I've been working on?

What can I do now that I couldn't do before?

What are the key things I still need to work on?

Where do you want to go?

Looking forward...

Where do I want my playing ability to be in 5 years?

_____

_____

_____

_____

_____

What would I like to be able to do in 12 months time?

_____

_____

_____

_____

_____

Which achievements are most important in the next 3 months?

_____

_____

_____

_____

_____

What's holding you back?

If I'm honest...

What are the key issues stopping me from getting better?

What are the main excuses I use for not taking action?

What will I regret most if I never reach my long-term goals?

How will you move forward?

In the next 3 months...

What key changes do I need to make?

_____

_____

_____

_____

_____

_____

Which central tasks do I need to focus on?

_____

_____

_____

_____

_____

What tools and resources do I need to help me?

_____

_____

_____

_____

_____

_____

The 3rd Quarter

Welcome to the third phase of your practice domination. There's plenty of work left to do, so let's get cracking!

Week 1

⏱ Exercise

Tasks	Goals
1)	
2)	
3)	

⏱ Learn

Tasks	Goals
1)	
2)	
3)	

⏱ Create

Tasks	Goals
1)	
2)	
3)	

Day	S	M	T	W	T	F	S
Time							

Focus Points:

_____

_____

_____

_____

_____

_____

_____

_____

_____

Week 2

Exercise

Tasks	Goals
1)	
2)	
3)	

Learn

Tasks	Goals
1)	
2)	
3)	

⏱ Create

Tasks	Goals
1)	
2)	
3)	

Day	S	M	T	W	T	F	S
Time							

Focus Points:

Week 3

Exercise

Tasks	Goals
1)	
2)	
3)	

Learn

Tasks	Goals
1)	
2)	
3)	

☺ Create

Tasks	Goals
1)	
2)	
3)	

Day	S	M	T	W	T	F	S
Time							

Focus Points:

Week 4

Exercise

Tasks	Goals
1)	
2)	
3)	

Learn

Tasks	Goals
1)	
2)	
3)	

⏱ Create

Tasks	Goals
1)	
2)	
3)	

Day	S	M	T	W	T	F	S
Time							

Focus Points:

Week 5

Exercise

Tasks	Goals
1)	
2)	
3)	

Learn

Tasks	Goals
1)	
2)	
3)	

⏱ Create

Tasks	Goals
1)	
2)	
3)	

Day	S	M	T	W	T	F	S
Time							

Focus Points:

_____

_____

_____

_____

_____

_____

_____

_____

_____

Week 6

Exercise

Tasks	Goals
1)	
2)	
3)	

Learn

Tasks	Goals
1)	
2)	
3)	

⏱ Create

Tasks	Goals
1)	
2)	
3)	

Day	S	M	T	W	T	F	S
Time							

Focus Points:

_____

_____

_____

_____

_____

_____

_____

_____

_____

Week 7

Exercise

Tasks	Goals
1)	
2)	
3)	

Learn

Tasks	Goals
1)	
2)	
3)	

⏱ Create

Tasks	Goals
1)	
2)	
3)	

Day	S	M	T	W	T	F	S
Time							

Focus Points:

Week 8

Exercise

Tasks	Goals
1)	
2)	
3)	

Learn

Tasks	Goals
1)	
2)	
3)	

⏱ Create

Tasks	Goals
1)	
2)	
3)	

Day	S	M	T	W	T	F	S
Time							

Focus Points:

Week 9

Exercise

Tasks	Goals
1)	
2)	
3)	

Learn

Tasks	Goals
1)	
2)	
3)	

⏲ Create

Tasks	Goals
1)	
2)	
3)	

Day	S	M	T	W	T	F	S
Time							

Focus Points:

Week 10

⏱ Exercise

Tasks	Goals
1)	
2)	
3)	

⏱ Learn

Tasks	Goals
1)	
2)	
3)	

⏱ Create

Tasks	Goals
1)	
2)	
3)	

Day	S	M	T	W	T	F	S
Time							

Focus Points:

Week 11

Exercise

Tasks	Goals
1)	
2)	
3)	

Learn

Tasks	Goals
1)	
2)	
3)	

⏰ Create

Tasks	Goals
1)	
2)	
3)	

Day	S	M	T	W	T	F	S
Time							

Focus Points:

Week 12

Exercise

Tasks	Goals
1)	
2)	
3)	

Learn

Tasks	Goals
1)	
2)	
3)	

⏱ Create

	Tasks	Goals
1)		
2)		
3)		

Day	S	M	T	W	T	F	S
Time							

Focus Points:

Week 13

Exercise

Tasks	Goals
1)	
2)	
3)	

Learn

Tasks	Goals
1)	
2)	
3)	

⏲ Create

Tasks	Goals
1)	
2)	
3)	

Day	S	M	T	W	T	F	S
Time							

Focus Points:

_____

_____

_____

_____

_____

_____

_____

_____

_____

Reflect & Plan

You're doing great!! Let's take another timeout to reflect on your progress, where you want to be, and what's holding you back.

Where are you at?

Based on the last 3 months...

What are the main things I've been working on?

What can I do now that I couldn't do before?

What are the key things I still need to work on?

Where do you want to go?

Looking forward...

Where do I want my playing ability to be in 5 years?

What would I like to be able to do in 12 months time?

Which achievements are most important in the next 3 months?

What's holding you back?

If I'm honest...

What are the key issues stopping me from getting better?

What are the main excuses I use for not taking action?

What will I regret most if I never reach my long-term goals?

How will you move forward?

In the next 3 months...

What key changes do I need to make?

_____

_____

_____

_____

_____

_____

Which central tasks do I need to focus on?

_____

_____

_____

_____

_____

What tools and resources do I need to help me?

_____

_____

_____

_____

_____

The 4th Quarter

Welcome to the fourth phase of your practice domination. Great work on making it this far. Keep it up!

Week 1

Date: _____ / _____ / _____

⏰ Exercise

Tasks	Goals
1)	
2)	
3)	

⏱ Learn

Tasks	Goals
1)	
2)	
3)	

⏱ Create

Tasks	Goals
1)	
2)	
3)	

Day	S	M	T	W	T	F	S
Time							

Focus Points:

Week 2

Date: _____ / _____ / _____

☼ Exercise

Tasks	Goals
1)	
2)	
3)	

◔ Learn

Tasks	Goals
1)	
2)	
3)	

⏲ Create

Tasks	Goals
1)	
2)	
3)	

Day	S	M	T	W	T	F	S
Time							

Focus Points:

Week 3

Exercise

Tasks	Goals
1)	
2)	
3)	

Learn

Tasks	Goals
1)	
2)	
3)	

⏱ Create

Tasks	Goals
1)	
2)	
3)	

Day	S	M	T	W	T	F	S
Time							

Focus Points:

Week 4

Exercise

Tasks	Goals
1)	
2)	
3)	

Learn

Tasks	Goals
1)	
2)	
3)	

☺ Create

Tasks	Goals
1)	
2)	
3)	

Day	S	M	T	W	T	F	S
Time							

Focus Points:

Week 5

Exercise

Tasks	Goals
1)	
2)	
3)	

Learn

Tasks	Goals
1)	
2)	
3)	

◔ Create

Tasks	Goals
1)	
2)	
3)	

Day	S	M	T	W	T	F	S
Time							

Focus Points:

Week 6

Exercise

Tasks	Goals
1)	
2)	
3)	

Learn

Tasks	Goals
1)	
2)	
3)	

⏱ Create

Tasks	Goals
1)	
2)	
3)	

Day	S	M	T	W	T	F	S
Time							

Focus Points:

Week 7

Exercise

Tasks	Goals
1)	
2)	
3)	

Learn

Tasks	Goals
1)	
2)	
3)	

⏱ Create

Tasks	Goals
1)	
2)	
3)	

Day	S	M	T	W	T	F	S
Time							

Focus Points:

Week 8

☼ Exercise

Tasks	Goals
1)	
2)	
3)	

◔ Learn

Tasks	Goals
1)	
2)	
3)	

◔ Create

Tasks	Goals
1)	
2)	
3)	

Day	S	M	T	W	T	F	S
Time							

Focus Points:

Week 9

☼ Exercise

Tasks	Goals
1)	
2)	
3)	

◔ Learn

Tasks	Goals
1)	
2)	
3)	

⏱ Create

Tasks	Goals
1)	
2)	
3)	

Day	S	M	T	W	T	F	S
Time							

Focus Points:

_____

_____

_____

_____

_____

_____

_____

_____

Week 10

Exercise

Tasks	Goals
1)	
2)	
3)	

Learn

Tasks	Goals
1)	
2)	
3)	

☺ Create

Tasks	Goals
1)	
2)	
3)	

Day	S	M	T	W	T	F	S
Time							

Focus Points:

Week 11

⏱ Exercise

Tasks	Goals
1)	
2)	
3)	

⏱ Learn

Tasks	Goals
1)	
2)	
3)	

☕ Create

Tasks	Goals
1)	
2)	
3)	

Day	S	M	T	W	T	F	S
Time							

Focus Points:

Week 12

Exercise

Tasks	Goals
1)	
2)	
3)	

Learn

Tasks	Goals
1)	
2)	
3)	

⏱ Create

Tasks	Goals
1)	
2)	
3)	

Day	S	M	T	W	T	F	S
Time							

Focus Points:

Week 13

☼ Exercise

Tasks	Goals
1)	
2)	
3)	

◔ Learn

Tasks	Goals
1)	
2)	
3)	

⏱ Create

Tasks	Goals
1)	
2)	
3)	

Day	S	M	T	W	T	F	S
Time							

Focus Points:

Resource List

Welcome to your resource list! When you need inspiration, here's a reminder of some great stuff you've discovered this year.

Recommended Reading

Recommended Listening

Recommended Viewing

Additional Resources

For more resources, including great free content, be sure to visit us at:

www.guitariq.com

Stay in touch with all the latest news. To connect with us online, head to:

www.guitariq.com/connect

Would you like to read more? For a complete list of our books, check out:

www.guitariq.com/books

Remember to grab your online bonus! Get the free bonus content for this book at:

www.guitariq.com/gn-bonus

Interested in a master class with us? To check out our online workshops, go to:

www.guitariq.com/academy

Liked This Book?

Did you find this notebook useful? You can make a big difference in helping us spread the word!

While it would be nice to have the promotional muscle of a major publishing house, independent authors rely heavily on the loyalty of their audience. Online reviews are one of the most powerful tools we have for getting attention and finding new readers.

If you found this book helpful, please consider helping us by leaving a review at your place of purchase. Reviews needn't be long or in-depth; a star rating with a short comment is perfect. If you could take a minute to leave your feedback, it would be sincerely appreciated!

Made in the USA
Lexington, KY
22 March 2019